SLEEP BUBBLES

Using mindfulness to help kids sleep

WRITTEN BY
HEATHER KRANTZ, MD

ILLUSTRATED BY
LISA MAY

Sleep Bubbles
Published by Herow Press
Bend, Oregon
herowpress.com

ISBN 978-0-9987037-4-9

First printing June, 2018

A Note to Parents and Caregivers:

Everyone experiences difficulty falling or staying asleep at some point in life. As adults this can be incredibly frustrating and can adversely affect health, emotions, memory, and the ability to function. Children are no different. Lack of adequate sleep can lead to moodiness, poor emotional control, inattention, and excessive tiredness. Kids may experience poor motivation, school problems, and behavior problems as well.

Children have little understanding of why this happens, and they do not have the tools to utilize to help them with sleep difficulties. As a parent and a doctor, I know that your child's sleeplessness can be a challenging problem for both of you. There are skills, however, we can we teach our kids to help them fall asleep or get back to sleep more easily.

A sleep routine is first and foremost. It is important to cease screen time, unplug, and move to quiet time early in the evening. Kids need a set bedtime. Consistency at bedtime is helpful including a quiet cool room, reading, and low lighting. Remember caffeine from earlier in the day in chocolate, chocolate milk, or soda can affect your child's ability to fall asleep. Young children need 10 to 13 hours of sleep daily (including naps) depending on age.

Beyond these bedtime practices, there are tools we can teach kids to assist them with sleep. Mindfulness is purposeful present moment awareness. It teaches how to pay attention to right now—not the future or the past. Mindfulness of the breath and body can help children let go of their busy minds and changing emotions and allow sleep to come. Awareness of happy thoughts and gratitude can also be helpful and easily understood by children. Giving kids these tools can empower them to take control of bedtime and inspire positive change.

Dedicated to my best friend Mar, who I love like a sister and who understands insomnia intimately.

Do you ever have a hard time
falling asleep?
Do you wake up and then
can't fall back asleep?

Me too.

Sometimes I'm thinking about exciting plans!

Or sometimes I'm worrying or feeling sad.

It seems like my mind is just so busy that it won't stop thinking!

BUZZ

It seems like there are busy bees in there buzzing.
They won't stop or be quiet.

BUZZ

BUZZ

But there are some ways
to help quiet those thoughts
so that you can sleep.

			1	2	3	4
5	6	7	8	9	10	11
12	13	14	15	16	17	18
19	20	21	22	23	24	25
26	27	28	29	30		

First, it is important to know that every day is different and every night is a brand new night. Tonight's sleep will be different from last night and tomorrow night.

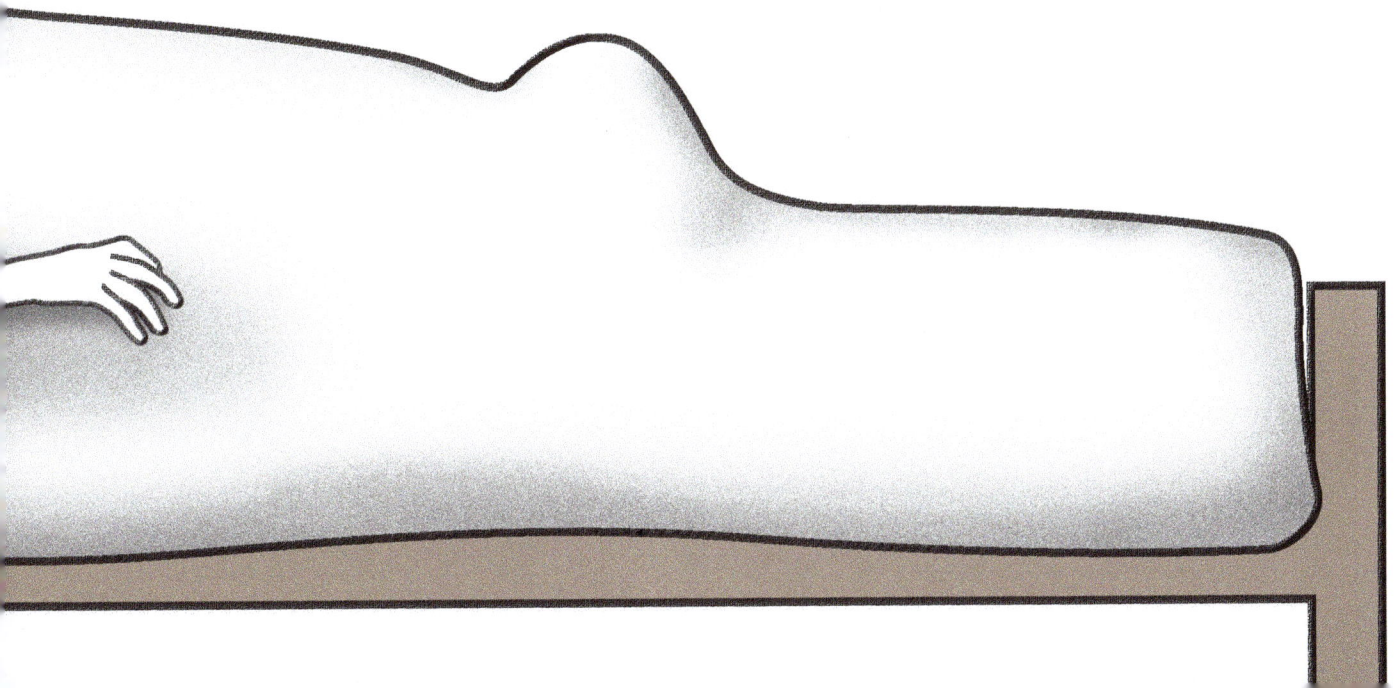

Also remember that sleep is good for us. It is how our bodies recharge—

just like rechargeable batteries.

We can give sleep some help by turning the lights down and getting all snuggly and quiet in bed.

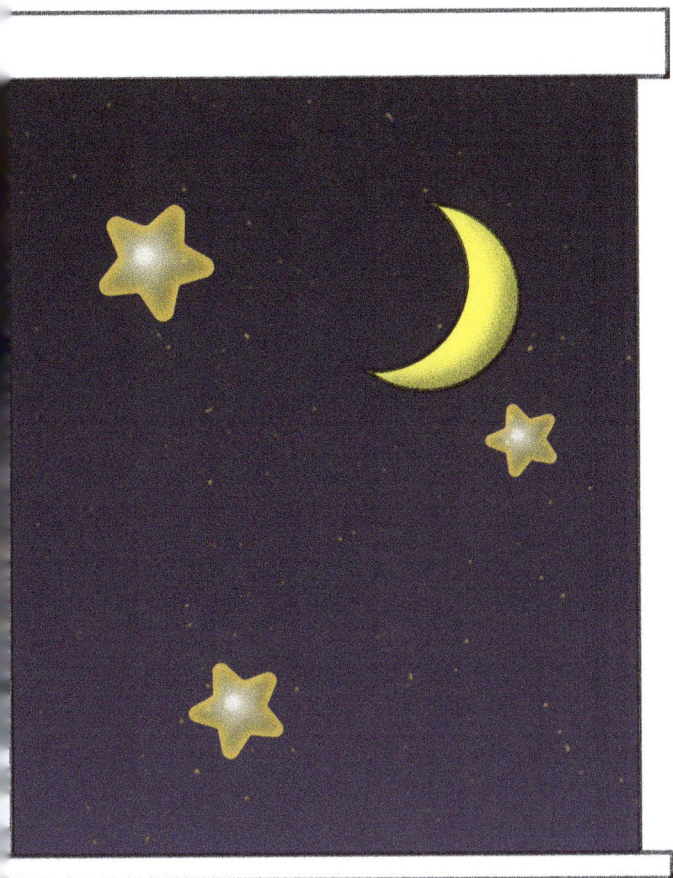

But we can't
force sleep
to come.
We have to stop
trying so hard.
Sleep just happens.

In order to
fall asleep,
we have to relax
and let go
of thinking.

Thoughts and feelings are like bubbles that come and go.
I call them mind bubbles.

When mind bubbles show up, you can
just let them be there until they go away
or change on their own.
Bubbles always pop or float away.

One helpful way to do this is with your breath. You can pay attention to your breath as it moves in and out of your body.

I just watch mind bubbles float away or pop while I'm noticing my breath.

Every time I have a
thought or feeling,
I tell myself, "Oh, I'm
thinking again."
And go back to
noticing my breath.

This really works!
(It's called mindfulness.)

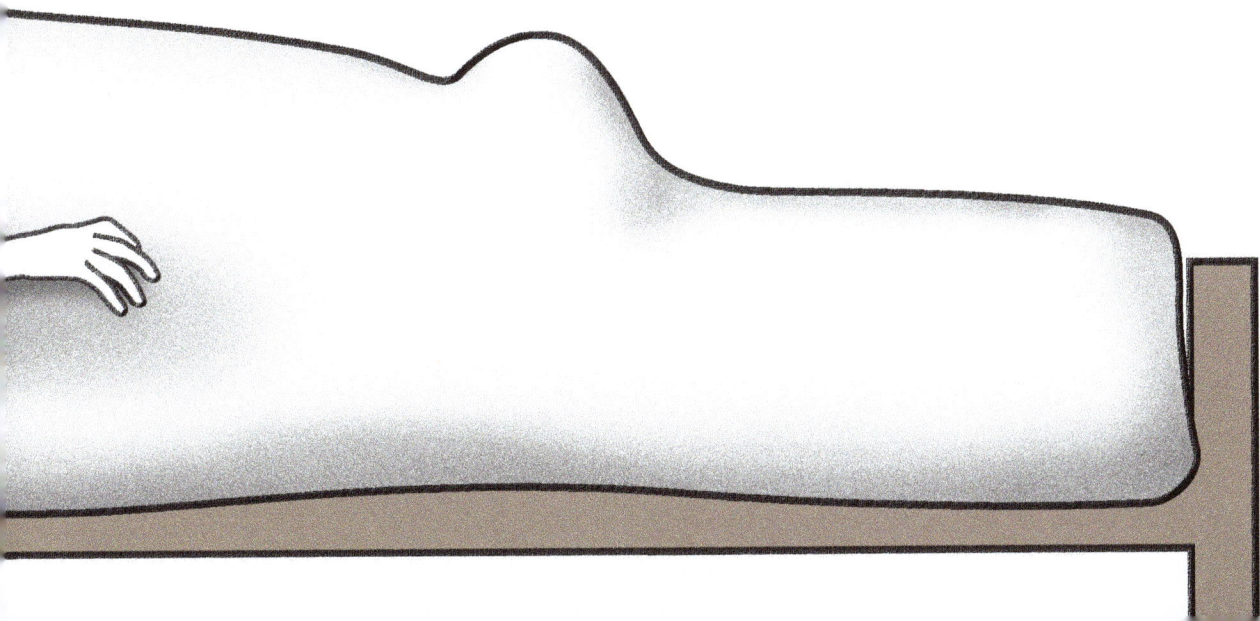

Something else that can help you
fall asleep is counting breaths.
I count 1 when I breathe in,
and 2 when I breathe out.
In 3 out 4, in 5 out 6, in 7 out 8,
in 9 out 10.

I hardly ever get to 10 before I have
to start over because
I forget what number I am on.
Or I fall asleep!

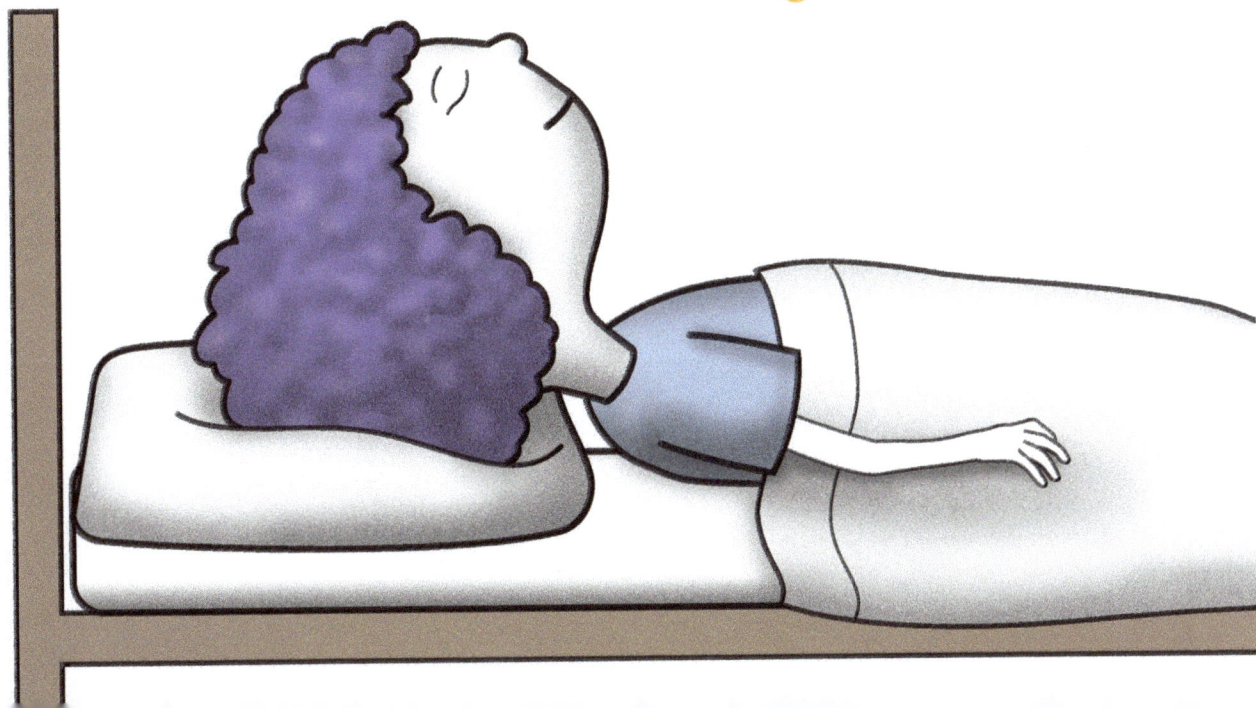

Another way that I sometimes fall asleep is by rocking one of my stuffed animals to sleep with my breath.

I put my teddy bear on my tummy and breathe him gently up and down. I think only about the movement of my breath and my tummy rocking Teddy to sleep. And sometimes I fall asleep with him!

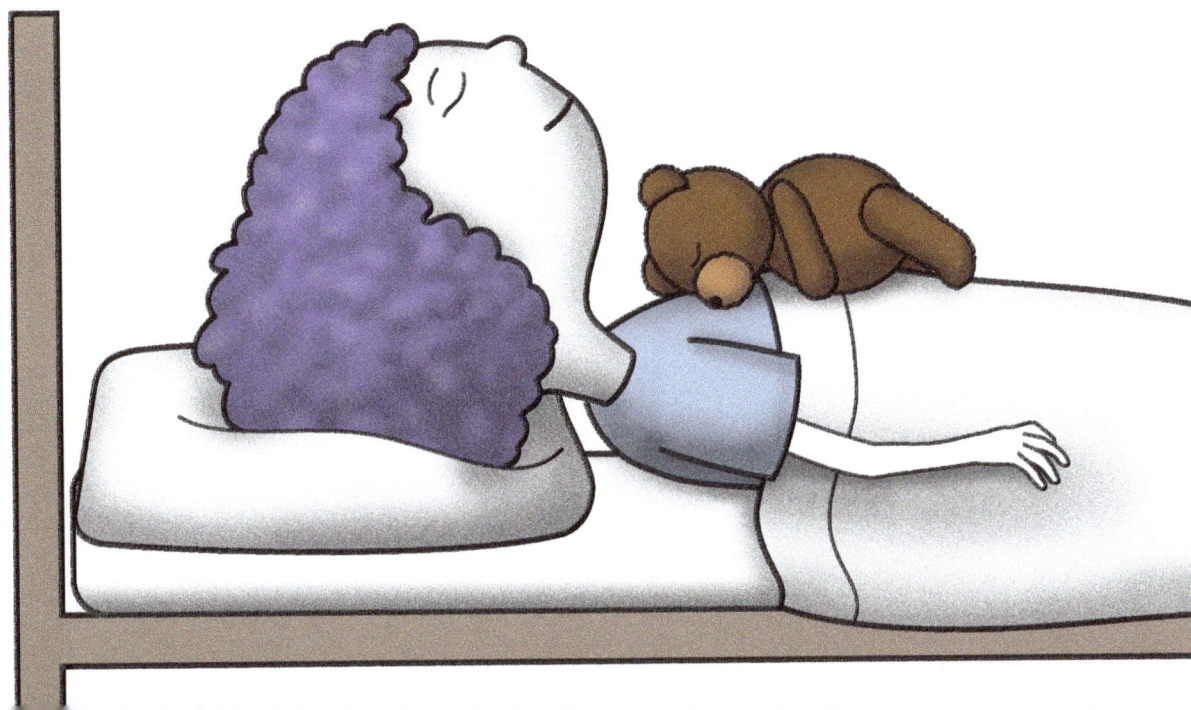

Here is another idea that helps me sleep. Sometimes I send happy wishes to everyone I love.

I LOVE YOU

THANK
YOU

Or I just say thank you
that they are in my life.
This is called gratitude.

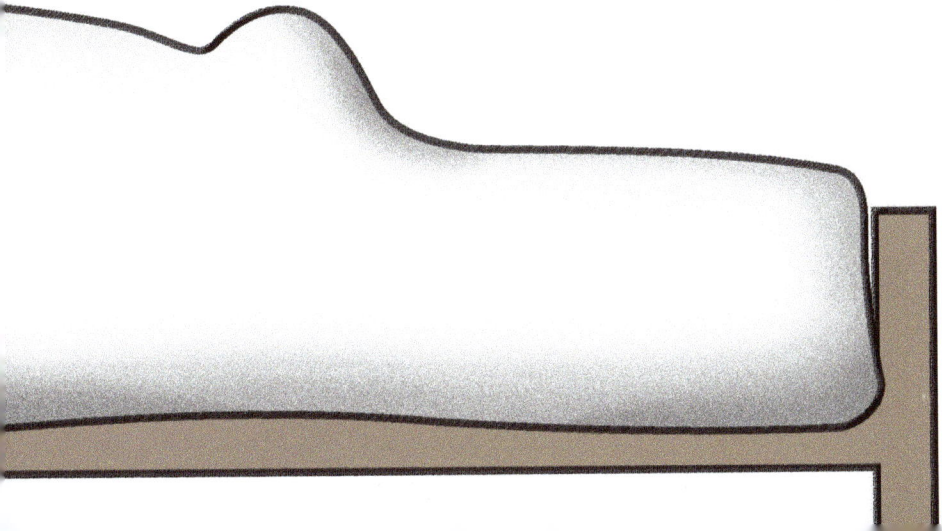

And here's my favorite way to fall asleep—it's called a body scan.

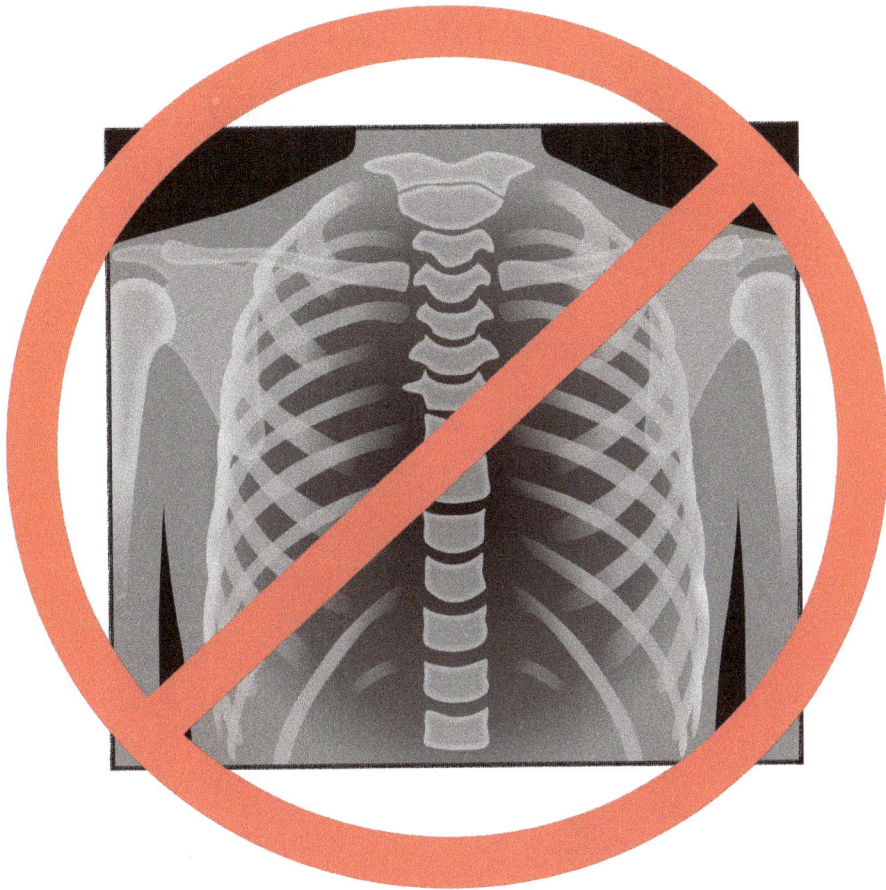

The name makes it sound like you are getting your whole body x-rayed, but you're not!

The body scan is a way to notice
how your body feels right now.
It's really simple.
I will teach you.

Start by paying attention to your feet.
Notice how your feet feel.
Do they itch or tingle
or feel hot or cold?
Or maybe you don't notice anything—
so just notice that there is no feeling.

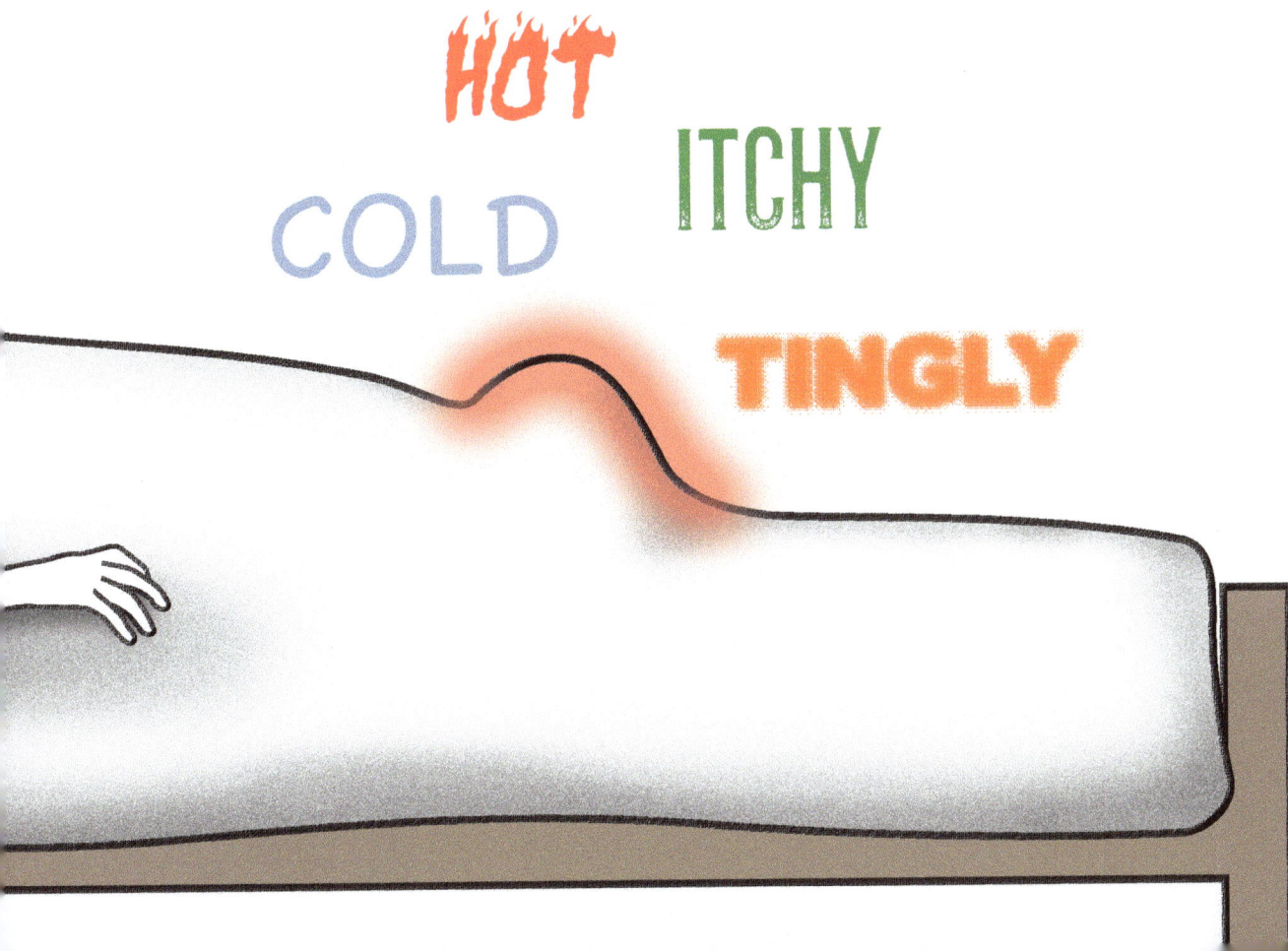

HOT

ITCHY

COLD

TINGLY

After a few breaths spent noticing your feet, move up to your legs and scan them. You can even imagine that different body parts have different colors!

If you get distracted by mind bubbles, just return your attention to the body part you are scanning.

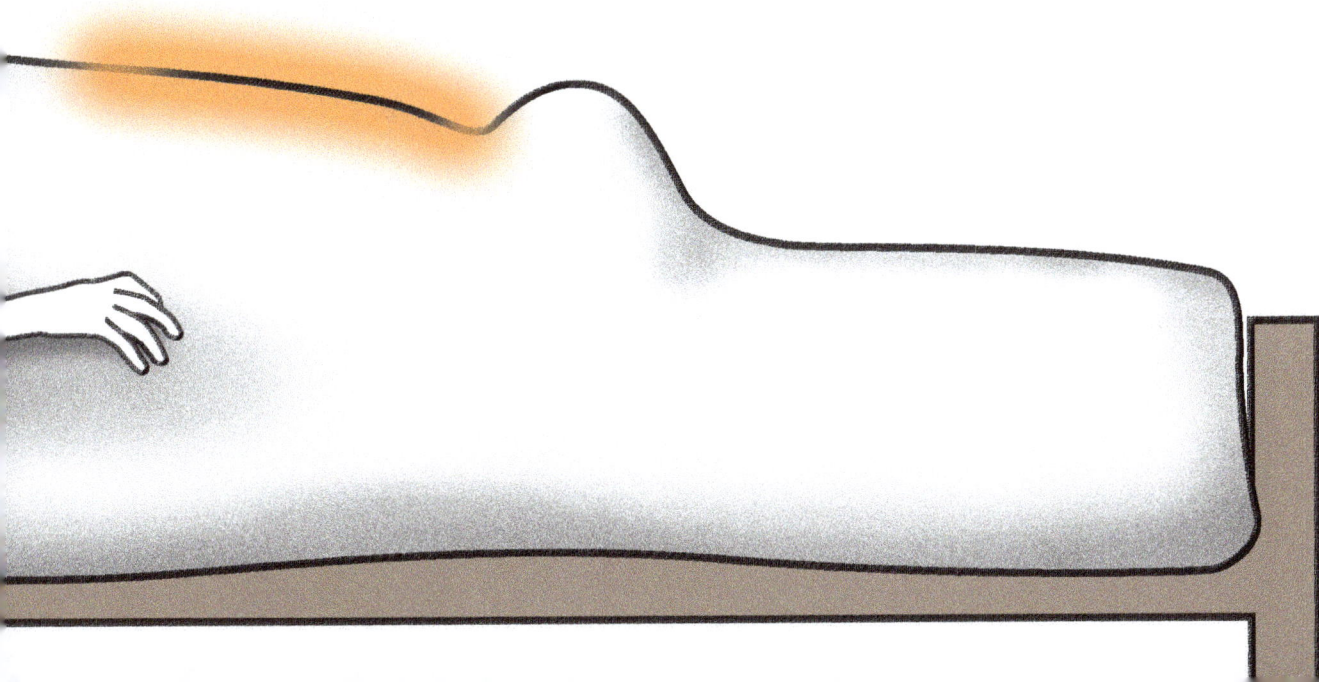

Try it now.
Notice your feet first.
Then after a few breaths,
move to your legs.
What do you notice?

After your feet and legs, continue
to scan up your body.
Next comes your tummy, then your
chest and shoulders...

and then your back, your arms, and your hands.

The last part to scan is your head
including your face.
Lots of times I fall asleep long before I
get to this part.

If I don't fall asleep, I usually feel more relaxed.
I lie there and accept that I'm awake right now, and that's okay.

I go back to noticing my breath moving in and out of my body.
I feel warm and safe in my bed and patiently wait for sleep to arrive.

But this doesn't happen much
any more now that I have
all of these new ways to help
me fall asleep!

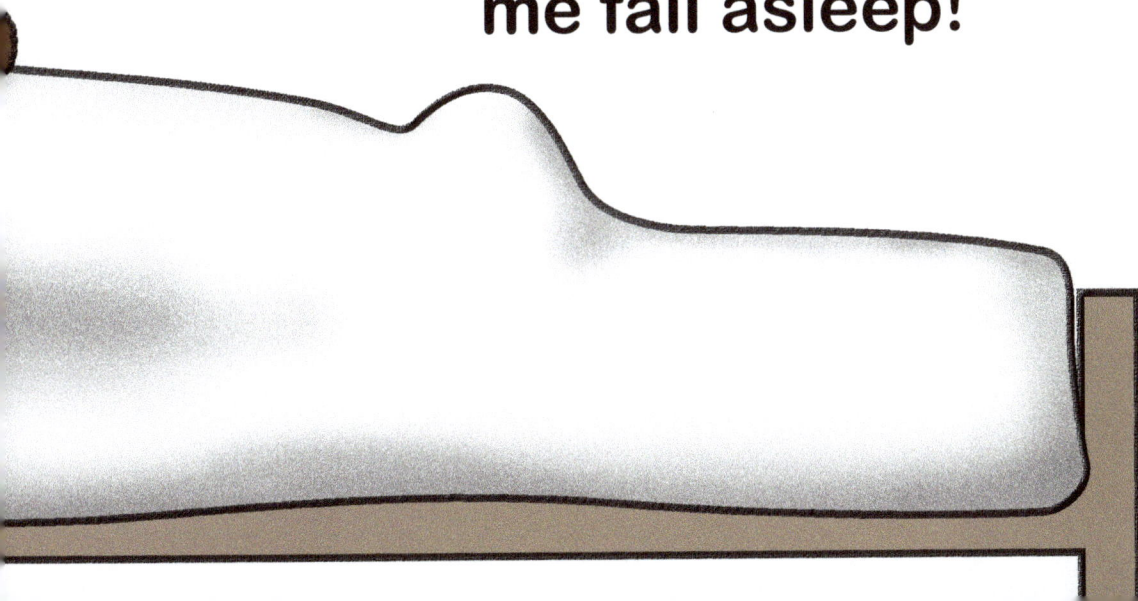

Be a sleep **STAR**!

Scan your body.
Take calm breaths.
Allow sleep to come.
Relax.

Guided Body Scan

(To be read by an adult and perhaps recorded for child to use when needed.)

Lying down on your back let your arms and legs fall to the side comfortably.

Close your eyes. Now take three gentle deep breaths and feel the air moving in and out of your body. You might feel your breath at your nose or in your belly. You can even put a hand on your tummy and feel it move up and down with each breath.

Now you are going to pay attention to different parts of your body.

Start with your feet. Notice whatever you feel in your feet. It might be itching or tingling, warmth or cold, or maybe nothing. That's okay. Whatever you notice is fine.

Now move your attention to your whole legs. Notice whatever feelings are present in your legs—your calves and shins, your knees, your thighs. If you start thinking about other things, just bring your attention back to noticing your legs.

Now move your attention up to your tummy. What do you notice there?

Next move your attention to your chest and shoulders. Every time your mind wanders off to something else, bring it back to noticing whatever part of the body we're scanning.

Now pay attention to your back.

Now move your attention to your arms. Notice your upper arms, elbows, lower arms, and wrists.

Next move to your hands. Bring your attention to whatever you feel in your hands.

And now move your attention to your head and face.

And last, pay attention to your whole body lying on your bed. You might notice your breath again moving in and out of your body.

And now just rest peacefully in the warm comfort of your bed.

Heather Krantz, M.D. is an integrative medicine physician and mindfulness teacher. She is the author of *Mind Bubbles: Exploring mindfulness with kids* and *Heart Bubbles: Exploring compassion with kids*. She trained as an obstetrician/gynecologist and completed a fellowship in integrative medicine. She now teaches Mindfulness-Based Stress Reduction, Mindful Self-Compassion, and mindfulness workshops and practices mind-body medicine in Bend, Oregon.

Find her at HeatherKrantzMD.com and InSightMindfulnessCenter.com.

Lisa May is a medical illustrator in Sisters, Oregon. She has a Masters of Science in Medical Illustration from the Medical College of Georgia. She has worked for nearly three decades illustrating and designing books, and she has a passion for children's books and reading with kids. She is the illustrator of *Mind Bubbles: Exploring mindfulness with kids* and *Heart Bubbles: Exploring compassion with kids*.

Find her at LisaMayStudio.com.

www.ingramcontent.com/pod-product-compliance
Lightning Source LLC
Chambersburg PA
CBHW040256100426
42811CB00011B/1285